ADVENTURES WITH IMPOSSIBLE FIGURES

ADVENTURES WITH IMPOSSIBLE FIGURES

BRUNO ERNST

TARQUIN PUBLICATIONS

Dedication

To Roger Penrose, who published the first notes on impossible figures in 1958 and who opened up a delightful field of experiment and investigation.

Acknowledgements

With thanks to Drs. N Lakeman for their encouragement and inspiration and to W.F.Veldhuysen, Cordon Art for permission to reproduce the works of M.C.Escher.

This book is the English version of the original book in Dutch entitled 'Avonturen met onmogelijke figuren' published by Aramith Uitgevers in 1985 and copyright Bruno Ernst. It was translated into English by the Ostermeier family, Pam, Jan, Elizabeth & Emma and Gerald Jenkins.

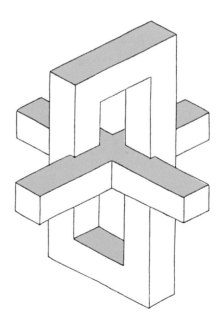

I.S.B.N.	0 906212 54 5	Tarquin Publications
© 1986	Bruno Ernst	Stradbroke
DESIGN:	PAUL CHILVERS	Diss
PRINTING:	THE HALESWORTH PRESS	Norfolk IP21 5JP
All rights reserved.		England

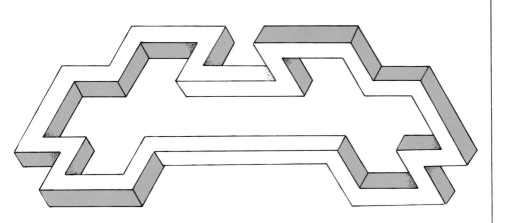

Contents

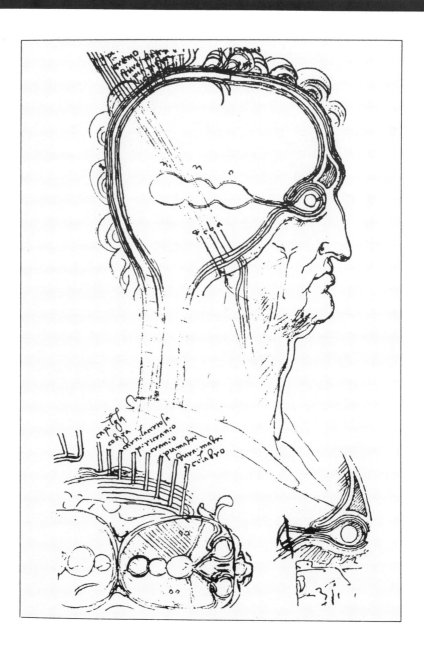

Leonardo da Vinci drew this cross-section of the head in about 1500. Although the anatomy of the brain itself shows little connection with reality, the relationship of the eye and the brain was clearly understood.

Real or Unreal?

This book is about the remarkable world of impossible figures. Figures which can be imagined or drawn, but which cannot be made in any concrete form. The impossibility is of a very special kind, existing and yet not existing, but also seeming to have a firm grip on the mind and on the imagination. It is not the impossibility of say a woman with a fish tail. Mermaids do not exist, but there is no problem imagining them, drawing them, or even making bronze or marble statues of them. Nor is it the impossibility of say a square circle. A square circle can neither be imagined nor drawn. The conflict between the word 'square' and the word 'circle' is so great that they cannot be dealt with simultaneously. No drawing is possible. The impossible figures we shall meet in this book are strangely imaginable and they can be drawn. That is what gives them their fascination and their attraction. They open up a new world, a world which intrigues the mind and which offers new insights into the nature of perception.

B.E. Utrecht.
July 1985

1. The Tri-bar

Let us make the acquaintance of our first impossible figure. What is it and what qualities does it have? We can see that this curious shape is made up of three bars, so for convenience let us call it a 'tri-bar'. What is a tri-bar?

To answer a question like that we have to deal with two separate layers of illusion. All we are really looking at is a set of lines printed on a piece of paper! Yet we appear to see a solid object. This first layer of illusion is so familiar that we may even hesitate to regard it as an illusion at all. Yet that is what it is.

Once we accept that first layer of illusion then it is plain that there is still a second layer to understand. What is this curious tri-bar?

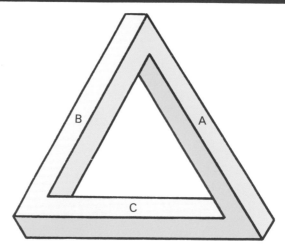

If we look carefully at the drawing, we can see that at the top corner, the bars A and B appear to be perpendicular. On the left, B and C are perpendicular. On the right C and A are perpendicular. How can this be?

The usual way to deal with a mysterious object is to try to understand it by examining it from different directions. This need not be done physically, it can be done in the imagination. If we see a box, a pencil or a teacup, then we can easily imagine how they would look from other directions without moving or touching them. An artist is perfectly able to sketch an object from one point of view while looking from another.

Can we do this with a tri-bar? What happens if we rotate it ?

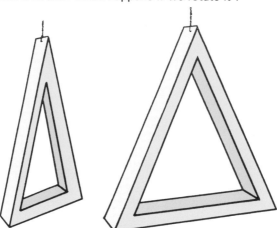

Are these two drawings views of a tri-bar as it rotates? Well, yes and no! Both at the same time! These drawings appear to represent nothing more than an ordinary triangular frame. The bars are no longer perpendicular and there would be no problem in making it out of wood or cardboard. At what point did the image disappear? Try to exercise your imagination by rotating the figure at the top of the page. What happens?

Here is a real photograph of an impossible tri-bar. No trickery. It is a real photograph.
Surely that proves that you *can* make an impossible tri-bar?

The complete photograph below shows that it is indeed possible to make an object from pieces of wood which when viewed from a certain angle appears to be an impossible tri-bar. The position of the camera is vital. To show how it is done, we have placed a mirror behind. In the mirror it is clearly seen not to be an impossible tri-bar at all.

The impossible tri-bar is indeed a strange and curious object, and one which we must investigate further.

The Eye

The organ which we call the eye is essentially a ball-shaped mini-camera. The lens focuses the image on the region at the back of the eye called the retina. This is made up of more than a hundred million light sensitive cells. From these cells more than a million nerve filaments carry the signals to the brain. These nerve filaments are bundled together as they leave the eye to make what is known as the optic nerve.

The signals transmitted along the optic nerve are processed in a specific part of the brain. This process is extremely complicated and barely understood, in spite of all the progress which has been made in recent years. However, for the purposes of this book, there is no need to be able to differentiate between the component parts. We shall call the whole visual process which allows an object or diagram in the outside world to be comprehended by the brain as the 'eye-brain combination' or simply as the 'eye-brain'.

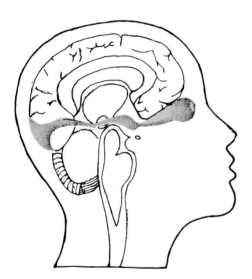

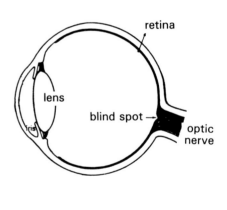

The combination of eye and brain which is able to process the visual information about the outside world is indicated in blue. Compare with Leonardo da Vinci's diagram on Page 6.

The image of objects in the outside world is focused by the lens on the retina. There is a small 'blind spot' where the optic nerve leaves the eye.

Is it Real?

With our eyes we are unable to observe directly the three-dimensional nature of the
world about us. First, the lens of the eye must focus a flat picture on the retina.
Then the brain must reconstruct an understanding of the three-dimensional reality.
You must not think that we are talking here about stereoscopic vision, which is the
effect of depth which we get by using two eyes. Even when we look with only one
eye we still get a good impression of the three-dimensional world.
The eye-brain combination is able to process a great deal of information and to
present the result in a fraction of a second. As human beings, we are able to walk
into a room and instantly recognise objects. We can say ''that is a chair, and there
is another one'', instantly drawing on our knowledge of the shape and colours of
chairs we have seen before and recognising them in any position. This is a
remarkable achievement and one which we are far from being able to imitate with
any computer. There is a kind of 'robot vision', where a combination of T.V.
camera and computer is able to distinguish between simple objects like cubes,
pyramids and cylinders when seen from any direction. However, it is only at the
most elementary stage of development and it will be many years before any such
combination will be able to approach the power of the human eye and brain.
It is clear that it does not matter whether we are looking either at the real three-
dimensional world or at a two-dimension representation in the form of a drawing or
a photograph. In either situation, the brain must process a flat image on the retina
in order to be able to understand what the eye is seeing. What actually happens
when we look at an impossible figure? What calculations does your brain have to
make when you look at the figures below?

Impossible tri-bar in a landscape.   Japanese tri-bar.

We are sure that you felt them to exist at the same time as you knew that they did not! There is a fundamental contradiction which cannot be resolved. You know that the bars which make up the impossible tri-bar cannot meet in real space, but the eye-brain still tries to assign a meaning. Millions of years of evolution have prepared the human brain to understand the real world, but it is now faced with an image which it cannot interpret. It knows that the shape cannot exist and yet the image does not then dissolve into a meaningless set of lines with no three-dimensional power. It seems possible to accept and reject it, both at the same time.

This gives the impossible figure a kind of real existence. It appears to have acquired a similar status to real objects like houses, trees and chairs, objects which the eye-brain has long been able to comprehend from the flat pictures on the retina. It is the curious real/unreal existence which is the intriguing characteristic of impossible figures.

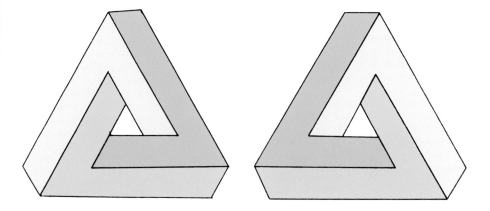

Tri-bars exist in pairs, each of which is a reflection of the other.

An Impossible Model ?

If you want to make a three-dimensional model of an impossible tri-bar, it is not necessary to use wood as I have done for the photograph on page 11. You can make a cardboard model. The net is given below and if you follow the instructions you will be able to make a three-dimensional object part of which will appear to be an impossible tri-bar when photographed or seen from a certain angle. Of course it is not really an impossible tri-bar. Impossible tri-bars really are impossible! The model needs to be strong, so you should make a photocopy of the page and then glue it to a piece of thin card before starting to make it up.

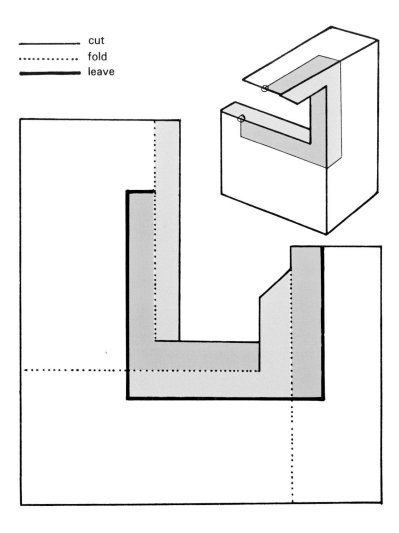

————— cut
············· fold
▬▬▬▬▬ leave

The Beginning

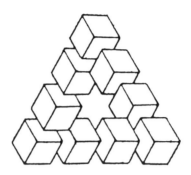

In the year 1934 the Swedish artist Oscar Reutersvärd drew this arrangement of nine cubes and the first impossible tri-bar had been created. He continued to experiment in this new field and made many hundreds of drawings. In 1958 L.S.& R.Penrose published a short article in the British Journal of Psychology : 'Impossible objects, a special kind of visual illusion'. In this article they described the impossible tri-bar and the idea of endless stairs. These ideas were taken up by other artists, especially Escher, and this fascinating subject became gradually known and appreciated by many more people.

In 1982 the Swedish Post Office commemorated the work of Reutersvärd by issuing a series of three stamps showing his impossible figures. In the same year a book was published which showed a selection of his drawings and it was later translated into several languages.

The graphic artist M.C. Escher has brought the knowledge of impossible figures to a much wider audience. His lithograph 'Waterfall', which he produced in 1961 makes use of three linked tri-bars in the centre of the print. He has brought out the contradiction in the impossible tri-bar in a most marvellous way. The water appears to flow steadily downwards and yet ends up higher than where it started. Reaching the top, the water spills out of its channel to form a waterfall which drives a waterwheel. Escher's brilliant imagination has used one impossibility, the tri-bar, to create another, the perpetual motion machine.

This has become one of Escher's best known and best loved of prints and more than 160,000 reproductions have been sold.

With the help of two drawings we can show that the impossible tri-bar really does have a special kind of existence.

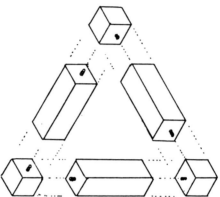

Here you can see how to construct a tri-bar. All you need are three small bars and three small cubes. The diagram looks most convincing. Most of us, even those who know it would not work, still feel that in some way it must be possible.

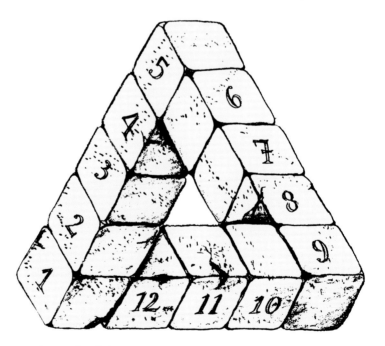

This diagram shows that it is even possible to calculate the volume and the surface area of an impossible tri-bar. Suppose that each cube is of side 1cm, then each side of the tri-bar is 5cm long. The volume is then 12cm^3 and the surface area is 48cm^2. Check it yourself. It is only a question of counting the number of cubes.

Tri-bar Fantasies

The impossible tri-bar can be used as a basis for all kinds of drawings. A few examples of the possible approaches are given on the next few pages.

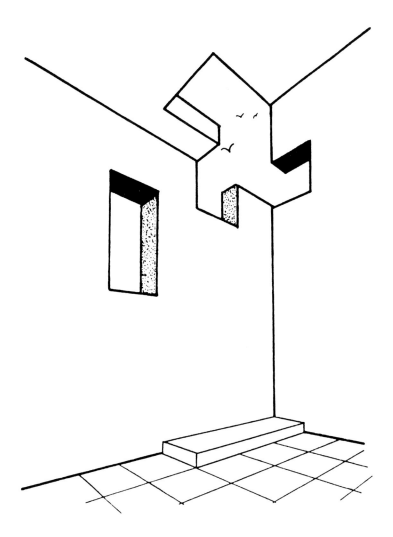

In 1984, I was asked to draw a jubilee poster for Oscar Reutersvärd to celebrate 50 years of impossible figures. This is the preliminary sketch. Note how the impossible tri-bar has disappeared to leave an impossible hole in the wall.

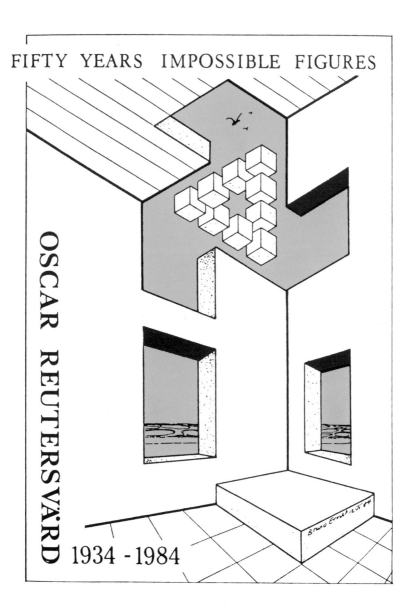

This was the jubilee poster. Reutersvärd's original figure, the one which started the impossible story, appears as an impossible heavenly body seen through an impossible opening in the wall!

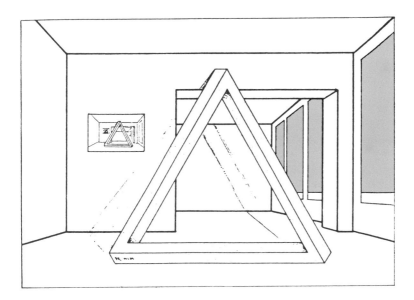

I tried to sketch an impossible tri-bar standing in the normal surroundings of the landing outside my flat, and then sent it to Oscar Reutersvärd.

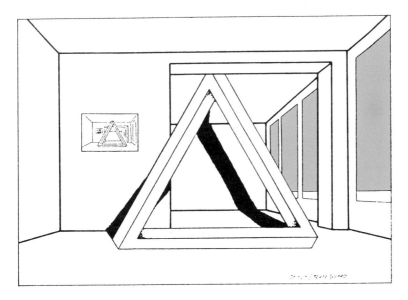

He sent it back a few days later, altered so that it was more interesting. The top of the tri-bar disappears behind the beam.

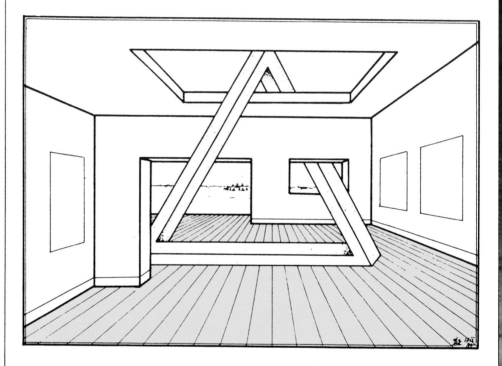

Inspired by this, I drew a third version in which a different kind of impossible figure (see chapter 7) is used to create a rather special kind of setting for the tri-bar. Now the room is a museum hall or possibly an art gallery, but one in which the placing of the model causes rather severe problems!

Perhaps in the year 2034, an impossible tri-bar will be erected on the moon to celebrate one hundred years of impossible figures. I borrowed the setting from Macaulay.

If ever the great pyramid of Cheops were to disappear then an impossible tri-bar of the same size could be placed on the site. It would use far less material.

In this chapter we shall discover that there are other curious impossible figures which tease the imagination just as wickedly as the tri-bar. We shall meet the impossible two-bar, a mysterious box which seems to contain real cubes, the impossible four-bar and so on. Can we carry this ever onwards to the five-bar, six-bar etc? And what about the impossible one-bar?

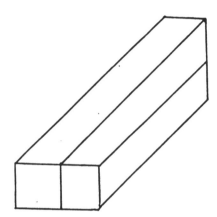

The Impossible Two-bar ?

The answer must be a double 'yes'. Yes, it is possible to draw an impossible two-bar and yes, it really is impossible!

The Mysterious Box

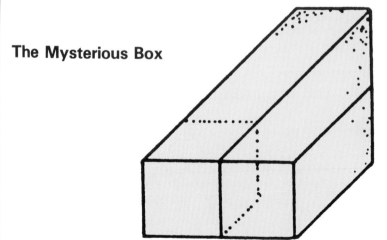

The Professor showed me a drawing of a mysterious box which he had made the previous day.

"Can you tell me how many cubes this box will hold?"

"To be honest I do not see it as a box at all".

"Perhaps I can show you how I got the idea and perhaps that will help you to see it".

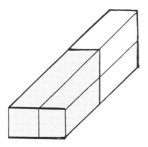

"First I drew an impossible two-bar and then sawed off some cubes from the far end. The shape which remains is the mysterious box. How many cubes does it contain?"

"I don't know. Could you draw how it looks from the back and the side for me?"

"Of course. The front is made up of two squares horizontally, but the back is two squares vertically. It looks like this."

The professor made two drawings and marked them 'back' and 'side'.

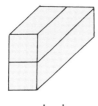

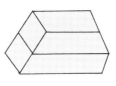

back   side

"I still cannot really see it, but I think there are more than four cubes. How many are there?"

"There are exactly five."

The professor could see that I was confused. He then drew an impossible tri-bar and moved the right hand bar further to the right. This made a new impossible figure.

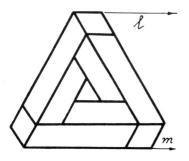

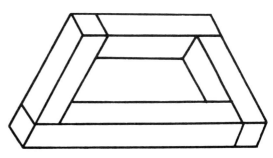

I could see that he had created a new impossible figure, a four-bar, but could not understand what it had to do with the mysterious box.

"How does that prove that your mysterious box contains five cubes exactly?"

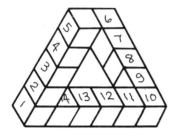

"Here is a four-bar which contains 14 cubes. I have numbered them to make it clear"

"Yes I can see that."

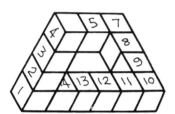

"Let us now remove cubes 5 and 6. This leaves a space into which we can put cube 5. Cube 6 is not wanted. This new shape needs 13 cubes."

"Yes, I understand, we need one cube less."

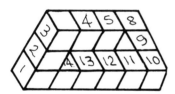

"Right I'll do the same again. Let us remove cubes 4,5,7. This leaves two spaces into which we can put cubes 4 and 5. Cube 7 is not wanted. This new shape needs 12 cubes."

"Yes, agreed."

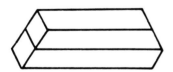

"Now you can see that if I go one stage further, the shape becomes an impossible two-bar. I haven't numbered it, but you must agree that it contains 11 cubes."

"Yes."

"Now take away six cubes from the right."

"And the shape which remains is your mysterious box, and it contains 11-6 = 5 cubes. Yes, at last I am convinced."

"I'm glad I have managed to convince you. There is an even smaller box which contains only 3 cubes, but most people cannot see it as a box at all." Can you?

The Impossible Four-bar

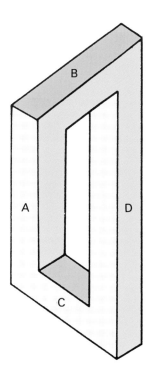

In the previous discussion we made acquaintance with a further impossible figure — the four-bar. It has two parallel bars and two which appear to cross each other perpendicularily.

As with the impossible tri-bar, the eye-brain immediately accepts it as a solid object — a kind of window frame which we know cannot exist, but which we cannot easily reject.

These diagrams show a perfectly normal window frame seen from two different directions. We can now see that the four-bar is an impossible combination of them both. Bars A and B are taken from the left diagram. Bars C and D from the right one. The result is confusion!

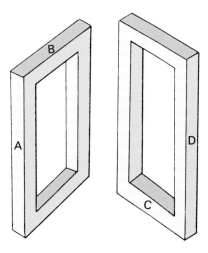

A Model of an Impossible Four-bar

This photograph shows on the right an object which appears to be an impossible four-bar, but the image in the mirror gives the secret away and shows how it was set up. You could make a model like this by glueing eight pieces of wood together or you could make the model opposite part, of which is an impossible four-bar.

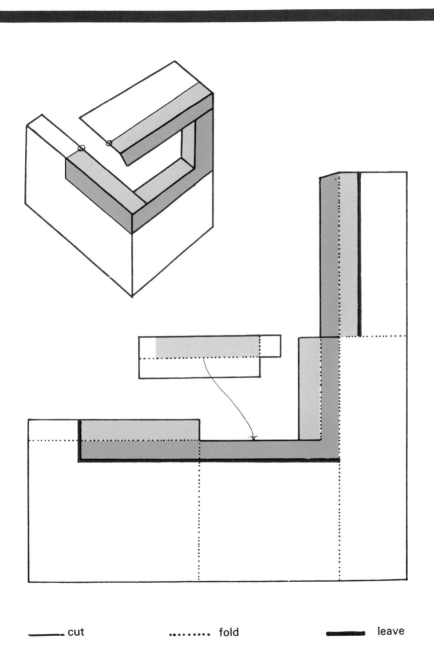

_____ cut   ········ fold   ▬▬▬ leave

As for the model on page 15, it is best to take a photocopy of this page and then glue it to thin card. You can use colour to strengthen the illusion.

"This wondrous object, standing far out in the desert, and built long ago by an unknown civilisation........"

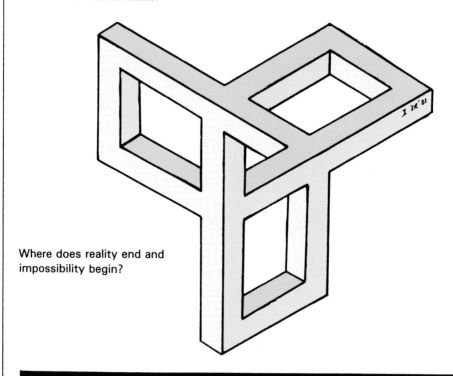

Where does reality end and impossibility begin?

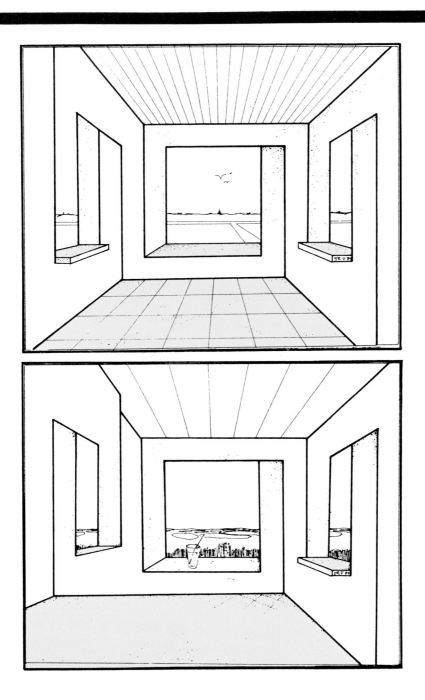

Strange rooms in palaces far away.

Real Corners and Impossible Frames

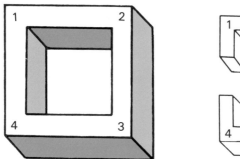

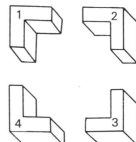

The drawing on the left represents a solid frame which is above and to the left of our view point. We can tell where it is, because we can make use of the clues given by the shapes of the corners. All four corners are different and we can easily see how different they are by drawing them separately. Drawing (b) shows the four types, which we number (1,2,3,4,), this time without shading.

It is possible to use these corners to make up other four-bars. Let us start with (1,1,1,1), which gives us a real four-bar seen from a viewpoint which is close to the frame and straight in front of it.

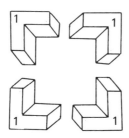

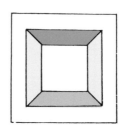

Below are the four-bars (1,2,1,2), (4,4,4,4), (4,1,4,1). All are impossible figures, with different kinds of impossibility.

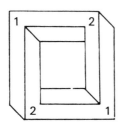

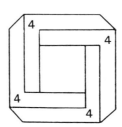

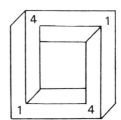

It is interesting to experiment with other combinations. Are the resulting four-bars real or impossible?.

Impossible Multi-bars

There is no problem in developing this idea further to generate impossible figures which have more than four bars. We can call them 'Impossible multi-bars'.
It would be reasonable to hope that one might be able to construct impossible figures which are even more interesting and more curious than those we have met so far. However that is not the case. There are two main reasons.

1. The image on paper which is percieved most strongly is that of a right-angled corner. The strength of the tri-bar and the four-bar is that all the corners appear to be right-angles. The angles at which the bars of multi-bars meet is greater than 90° and the greater the angle the less secure is the grip on the mind.

2. Complexity. The more lines and bars there are in the drawing the less the contradictions may be noticed.

To draw impossible multi-bars we can use the same method as we used for the four-bar and experiment by joining corners of different types.

An impossible five bar.

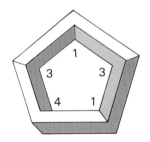

This impossible figure is (1,3,1,4,3).

An impossible six-bar.

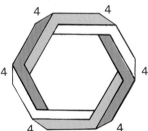

This impossible figure is (4,4,4,4,4,4).

An Impossible Infinity Bar ?

Just as a circle can be seen as a polygon with an infinity of sides, so we can create a rounded impossible figure. Or is it really a rounded two-bar which we could describe as (4,4)?

This impossible figure has been worked into several beautiful pictures by Sandro de Prete. You can also see it in impossible alphabets where the rounded shape comes in very useful.

Impossible Mono-bars

Most people find it suprising that impossible mono-bars can exist at all. However, they can, and here are two examples.

It is likely that you will find both of these drawings rather disappointing. Most people do. The eye hardly detects anything suspicious and is willing to interpret both drawings simply as bars which have been sawn off at a slant. Look carefully though, and you will see that both are indeed impossible mono-bars.

Below is a much more interesting version which was created by Zenon Kulpa. On the left it seems to be two distinct bars. On the right there is only one. It seems that the second bar is almost entirely created out of the first and its shadow. So there is no second beam at all.

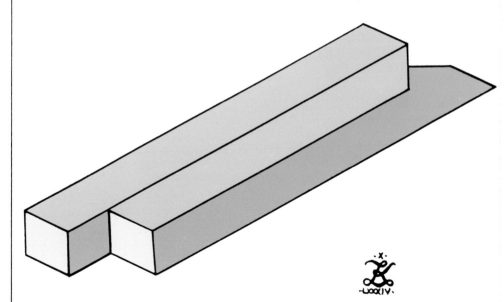

Perhaps we should call it 'a beam and a half'!

Enter Through Closed Doors.

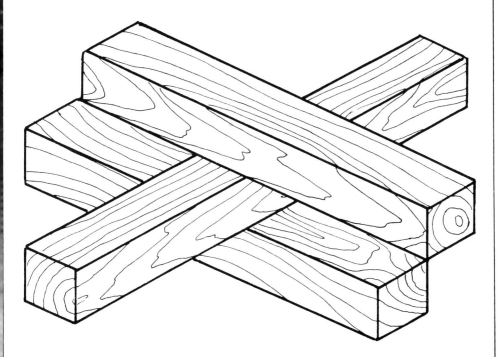

This ingenious impossible figure manages to combine three regions, each strongly acceptable to the eye. On the left and right two beams appear to touch along an edge. In the centre a third beam passes between the other two. Yet they are the same two beams which have no space between them. A fairy-tale has come true. One can enter through closed doors!

3. Misleading Signposts

An impossible figure exists because the visual signposts and clues which tell us about its position in space give contradictory information. So far we have met and used various indicators, mostly without really being aware that we have done so. But there are three main signposts which we use, quite unconsciously in most instances.

1. The covering and joining of planes.

2. The continuity of planes.

3. The orientation of planes.

Later we shall deal with the continuity of planes in more depth, but for the moment the context will offer sufficient explanation. Let us examine how these three types of misleading signposts can operate, individually and in combination.

1. Covering and Joining.

These three illustrations of crossed bars draw attention to what we unconsciously interpret about the positions of the bars

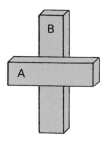

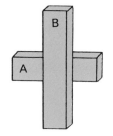

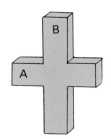

(a) A is in front of B because B is covered by A

(b) A is behind B because B covers A.

(c) A and B are the same distance away because we can see that A and B join.

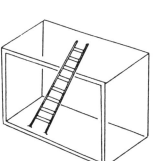

(d) Here we can appreciate the power of misleading signposts to lead our minds astray. The ladder begins inside and ends outside. It is an impossibility. But it is an impossibility simply because of one indicator. The ladder appears to pass in front of the top line. Without that, there would be no unresolved conflict and no impossibility.

2. The Continuity of Planes

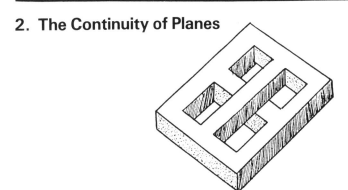

This impossible figure springs to life because we have used two different indicators of position at the same time. Around the perimeter the continuity of planes tells us that the top is flat. But in the centre one beam passes in front of the other. There is conflict and so an impossible figure is born.

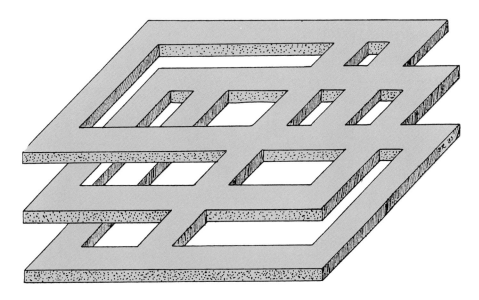

The confusion can be made stronger still by adding further three-dimensional signposts of relative position. If we look at the left side of this figure there are three layers, apparently one above the other in a vertical line. This is further reinforced by the crossing of one layer above another as far as the centre. But on the right side the visual signposts all point to a single plane. The mind is delightfully confused.

Of course there are many different versions of this type of figure and it is interesting to combine these ideas with those of the impossible four-bars from chapter 2.

3. The Orientation of Planes

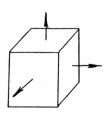 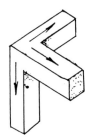

The eye seizes on any opportunity to comprehend the orientation of planes. On the left we can see how a cube immediately defines three perpendicular directions in space, directions which the eye expects to be maintained consistently across the whole illustration. On the right, three bars meeting at a corner define the directions even more strongly.

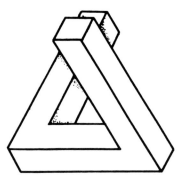

This figure causes no problems. The planes firmly define three directions in space and one bar passes in front of the other just as we expect.

Here there are problems. The directions are clearly defined, but in both cases the orientations are not maintained across the whole figure. The signposts of covering and joining give different information from the signposts of orientation. The result is that we have two different impossible figures. At this point we can admire once again the elegance and simplicity of the impossible tri-bar.

4. Perceptual Inversion

Let us leave our search for further kinds of impossible figures for the moment and investigate a closely related phenomenon called perceptual inversion. There exists a family of figures which the eye-brain combination can interpret in two or more ways and then be persuaded to switch between them.

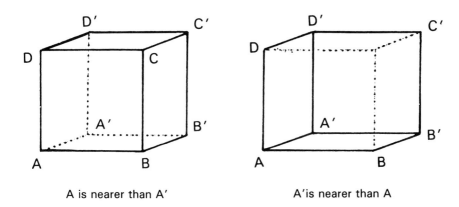

A is nearer than A'   A' is nearer than A

These two sketches of a cube are identical in size, position and lettering. They differ in that certain lines are strengthened or weakened. The result is that on the left we see a cube which is below and to the left of our viewpoint whereas on the right we see a cube which is above and to the right. There is no ambiguity.

The Necker Cube

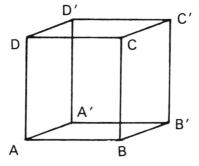

This third cube is identical in size, position and lettering but all 12 lines are drawn with equal emphasis. It is called "The Necker Cube". Are we looking at it from above or from below? Do you agree that it could be either? It is an ambiguous figure. If you find it hard to switch between the two possible viewpoints, then look carefully at the two sketches above. The phenomenon of switching between the two interpretations is called perceptual inversion.

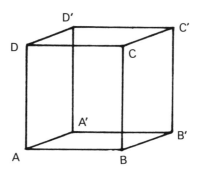

When we look carefully at the Necker Cube and are able to switch at will between the two interpretations, it is interesting to see what happens to particular lines and planes. They do not all change in the same way. For instance DD' changes in orientation is space as D and D change places but AD remains parallel to itself. AD changes in position, but not in orientation, but DD' changes in both position and orientation. It is worth investigating what happens to BB' and to the planes ABCD and BB'C'C as the perceptual inversion takes place.

The change in orientation of the lines in the Necker Cube depends very much on the viewpoint from which the cube is drawn.

(a)   (b)

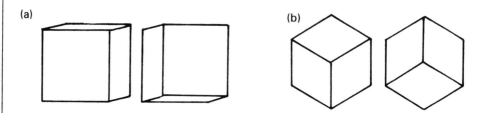

The angle of change is very small when the cube is drawn so that it inverts between the two positions on the left. On the right the angle is as great as it can be. The drawing on the right compares with the top right of the dice pictures opposite.

The Necker Cube with the greatest angle of change is the one which is a combination of the two drawings in (b). They combine to give a hexagon and the centre of the cube is directly behind A in both states of inversion. We can even calculate the angle through which it rotates. Let us now consider a little experiment with two cubical dice.

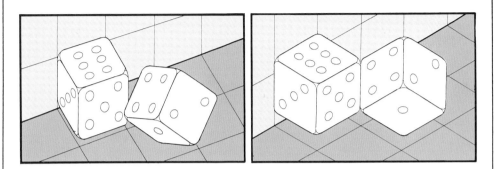

These drawings are of the *same* configuration of two dice but from two different view-points and they closely parallel the ideas of perceptual inversion. The drawing on the left shows that the two cubes actually touch at a single point. However, the drawing on the right shows that choosing a particular view-point can make the edges appear parallel. Also the right cube appears to lean backwards or even appears to be inverted. It is interesting to experiment with two cubes to obtain this effect.

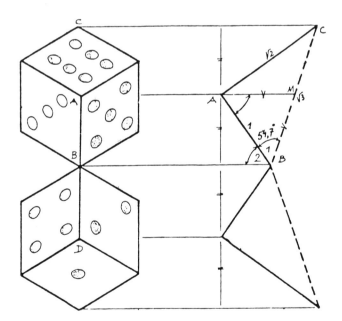

To calculate the angle which the edges make with each other to create this effect, it is best to move the right hand cube down so that its top corner corresponds with B, not turning or twisting it as you do so. Then the angle ABD is twice the angle ABC. From the section on the right we can calculate that ABC is 54.7°. Hence the angle ABD is 109.5°.

Concave and Convex

When we look at a Necker Cube we are accepting a convention which allows us to see inside the cube to the edges behind. Suppose we now leave out those hidden edges and draw only the 9 edges which could be seen on a solid cube. It can be drawn either way up and in either case there is ambiguity.

CONVEX

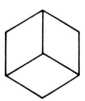

1. It is a solid cube seen from above.   2. It is a solid cube seen from below.

CONCAVE

3. It is a drawing of the 3 inside faces   4. It is a drawing of the three inside
of a cube seen from below.   faces of a cube seen from above.

Most people see the convex form straight away and have some difficulty in seeing the inverted form. To make it easier we need more visual signposts.

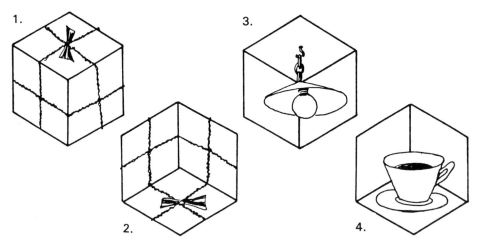

These four drawings show how much easier it is to accept that the cube shape is concave or convex, once other details and visual clues are added.

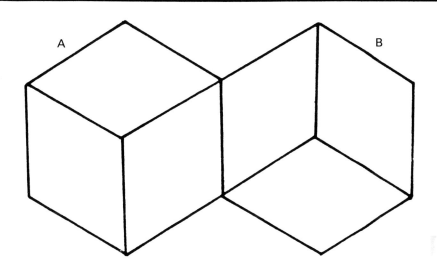

This figure is an abstraction of the dice drawing on page 40 and is also the figure created when the two versions of the cube on the page opposite slide together to share a common edge. Since either A or B can be concave or convex we have four possibilities.

1. A is concave and B is concave.

2. A is concave and B is convex.

3. A is convex and B is concave.

4. A is convex and B is convex.

We can then ask ourselves the following questions.

1. Which interpretation is seen first ?

2. Which inversions will take place spontaneously and which are difficult?

3. When the orientation of one half is fixed is it easy to carry it over into the other half? Is it true that interpretations 1 and 4 are the easiest to see?

Speaking personally, I see 4 most easily. For me the convex form dominates. Next I can see 2 and 3 and only with great difficulty can I see 1. Perhaps you found on Page 40 that the spots on the dice made any interpretation except 4 very difficult in spite of the problem with the unexpected orientation.

The Conflict of Two Orientations.

In this chapter we have not so far mentioned impossible figures. Each of the two views of the Necker cube excludes the other and so we have alternative views, not impossibility. We now ask ourselves if it is possible to combine both views in some way in order to create an impossible figure. Can we add details which force one view on one plane and the other on another ?

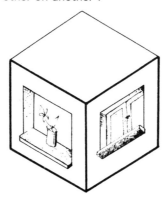

This figure shows an attempt to do this. If we concentrate on the left side the shape of the window forces a convex interpretation, whereas on the right it tries to force a concave interpretation. However, I think you will agree that it does not really seem to establish itself as a pleasingly stable impossible figure.

The central part of Escher's print 'Concave and Convex' is shown opposite and it also has a similar construction. Isolated from the print we cannot perceive it as a stable impossible figure. Escher's interpretation was to make us experience inversion in a jerky way as we pass from left to right across the drawing.'Concave and convex' makes us experience inversion as a movement, not as a static and stable unresolved conflict.

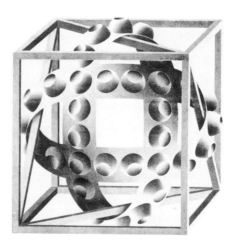

The print 'Cube with Boards' also by Escher (1957) presents the same problem.

The middle section of the print 'Concave and Convex' by Escher(1955).

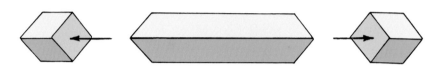

We first met this figure on page 34 in the search for a convincing impossible mono-bar. Although it is indeed an impossible mono-bar, the eye is still willing to regard it as a real bar with slanting ends. Even when we cut a cube from each end and so show the different orientations, most people still find it rather unsatisfactory.

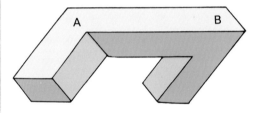

However, matters can be improved if we add to the cubes at either end. This figure shows the result. In my opinion it is a true impossible figure. Going from A to B forces us to switch orientation and then to accept it. It is impossible and yet it is stable and convincing at every point.

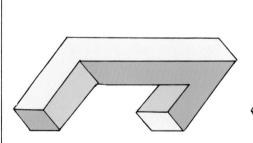

Going one stage further forces a second change of orientation.

Finally we can create a closed framework rather like those in chapter 2.

So it really is possible to develop stable figures which force us to accept contradictory orientations.

Both figures on the page opposite force contradictory changes of orientation on the eye. The upper diagram is an impossible figure. The second shows how the ends of the bars can be modified to increase the strangeness. Note how it has also created squares at the centres of all three faces.

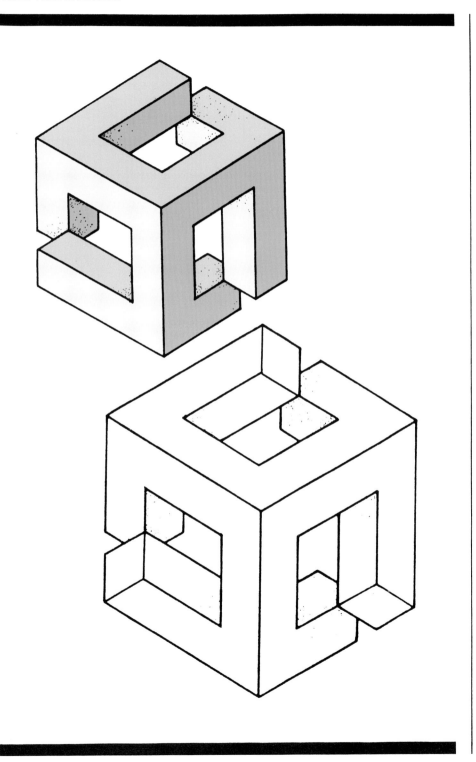

The Thiéry-Figure

(a) 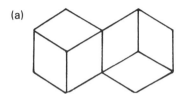   (b)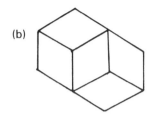

On page 43 we slid two cubes together so that they shared a common edge and obtained a rich source of figures and investigations. Now we can slide them even closer together so that they share a common face. This is shown in diagram (b). This figure was thought of by A.Thiéry at the end of the last century. It is not an impossible figure.

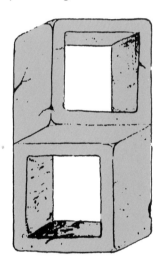

We could do an investigation of the concave-convex relationship as we did for figure (a), but there is more to be discovered. Firstly, it is rather stable. See the drawing on the left. This is rather remarkable because it suggests that the dividing line between unstable inversion figures and stable impossible figures is not all that great.

A number of artists have been used the Thiéry-Figure as a basis to generate illusions which seem remarkably stable. In particular Tsuneo Taniuchi, who designed a strange double alphabet, of which the three letters H, S and T are given below.

 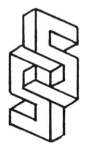 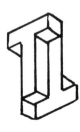

The whole alphabet was printed in 'Upper and Lower Case' Vol 10 No 3, September 1983 in the International Journal of Typographics.

A Curious Model

It is interesting to make this curious and little known model which was suggested to me by Professor J.B. Deregowski. It is a kind of truncated pyramid,which is neither impossible nor ambiguous,but held in certain ways it looks three-dimensional in a quite different way from its actual shape. Turn your model so as to minimise the number of faces you can see at the same time.

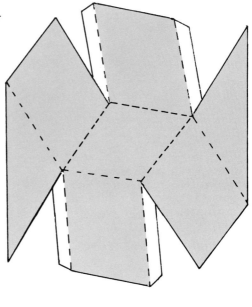

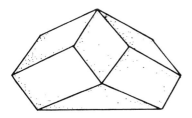

Trace or copy this plan and then make it up. Without a base it works quite well, but you might prefer to add one later to give it extra strength. Draw thick black lines along all the creases.

—— cut
- - - fold

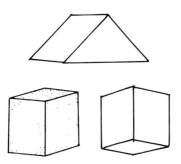

Here are three possible views of the model.

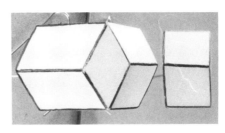

Here is a photograph of the model and its image in a mirror.

It is well worth holding your model in front of a mirror to reproduce the effect in the photograph. Does colouring the faces improve or reduce the illusion?

5. Impossible Cuboids

On page 33 we noticed that multi-bars were mostly less effective when the number of lines in the figure became too great. This disadvantage becomes less serious when the overall design reminds us of some well-known form. Our brains seem to be very good at recognising shapes which are similar to those seen before and then noticing small changes.

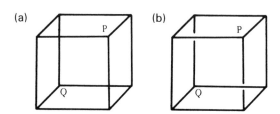

(a)   P   Q   (b)   P   Q

We saw in the last chapter that cuboids of the type given in (a) which are made up of 12 solid lines can be interpreted in two different ways. We are given no information about which line passes in front of which other so there is ambiguity. We can cheat a little, as we have done in (b), and leave a gap in two of the lines. This small change tells the eye that certain lines are nearer. This suggests that P and Q are both the same distance from the observer. An impossibility ! But convincing, I hope you will agree.

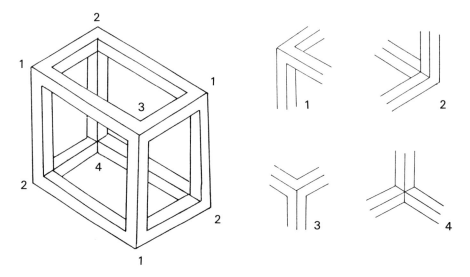

The drawing of the cuboid above is made up of solid bars and so no such ambiguity or cheating is possible. You will see that there are four different kinds of corner and they are sketched separately on the right. The corners of types 1 and 2 alternate round the edge of the diagram and types 3 and 4 are found near the centre.

We can then try to devise new kinds of cuboid by placing different types of corner in different positions.

This impossible cuboid uses the corner of type 1 six times round the edge and two corners of type 3 near the centre.
It forms a strange shape with the curious property that the visible planes form a continuous ribbon. Try tracing a path along them.

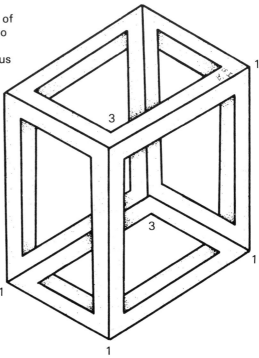

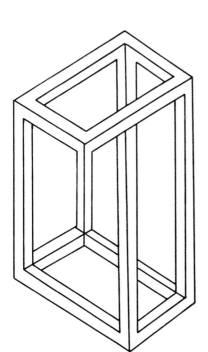

This impossible cuboid is one of a class where the vertical edges have different lengths.

This postage stamp, showing an impossible cuboid, was issued on the occasion of the Tenth International Congress for Mathematics in 1981.

Escher's Belvedere

Some impossible cuboids are too strange for the eye to accept. There may be too many contradictory visual signposts for the eye-brain to come up with a satisfactory interpretation. At this point the drawing collapses into a meaningless collection of lines. To create a successful figure the artist must strengthen some visual clues and weaken others. Then the contradiction between the possible and impossible can create an image which is both intriguing and memorable.

Maurits Cornelis Escher was a master of this art. Let us take a closer look at his print 'BELVEDERE' (1958) on the opposite page. It is based on the impossible cuboid, but so subtley treated that the cuboid itself is scarcely visible

(a)

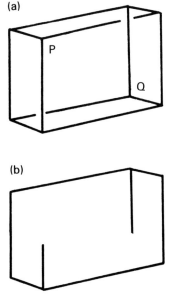

(c)

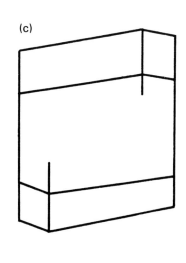

(b)

The impossible cuboid is long and narrow and the points P and Q are not far from the edge. This means that there is a relatively large open space in the centre. The most surprising thing is that P is invisible and Q is unobtrusive. Yet they should be the most important points to make us accept the cuboid as real and unreal at the same time. By diminishing some lines as in (b) and then breaking up the outline of the cuboid with an arcade and a ballustrade Escher has weakened the centre. The heavy and detailed construction above and below the weakened centre has strengthened the conflict See (c). We get the impression that the top and bottom planes cross each other perpendicularly and this is emphasized by the directions in which the woman on the top floor and the man on the right are looking.

'Belvedere' by Escher (1958)

To connect the top and the bottom planes needs a minimum of four pillars, of which the two on the outside cannot contribute to the illusion of impossibility. Escher used eight pillars and six of them contribute to the illusion. Investigate the ends of each pair which make an arch! In doing this he more than compensates for the original loss sustained by camouflaging the points P and Q. And finally there is the ladder which is inside and outside at the same time. This is the absurdity which most people notice first about the print.

At first Escher's work was not taken seriously by art critics and historians. But gradually it became more and more popular and now he is accepted as an artist of the first rank with a unique, rather surrealist style. From his handling of the impossible cuboid in 'BELVEDERE' we can see how effectively he was able to use his vivid imagination to demonstrate his delight in the representation of the impossible. A delight we can all share.

Cuboids with Strange Connections.

The cuboids which we have met so far have had all their corner points joined by beams or lines. However, we find we can make quite a lot of changes without losing the overall impression of a cuboid.

For instance, we can allow some corners to be connected, not to other corners, but to points on the opposite side. For instance a corner could be connected to the middle of a beam opposite. We can experiment with different shadings and unexpected coverings and joinings, some of which produce figures of particular interest. Below are some examples of the kinds of figure we can create.

Unfinished Symphonies

If we remove three of the twelve bars which make up a cube, the eye can still comprehend it as a cube shape. There is no difficulty in the diagram on this page in seeing and accepting the existence of planes in three directions at right angles to each other. The outline and the position of the viewpoint are the same as those of cubes in chapter 4 which could be inverted at will. However, on this page the sense of solidity is so strong that it is only with the utmost difficulty that any sense of inversion can be maintained for more than a few seconds at a time.

On the page opposite are two figures developed from this one. Notice how the bars have been modified to alter the coverings and their orientation. This field is a rich one for further experiments and there are many interesting variations to discover.

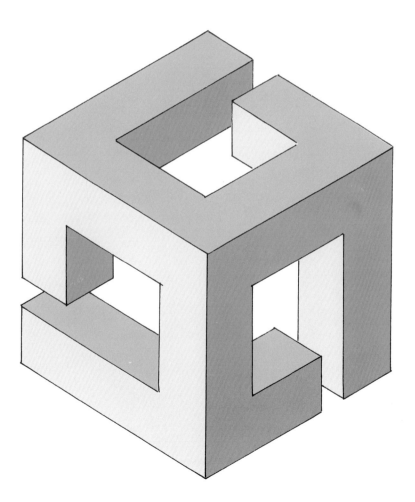

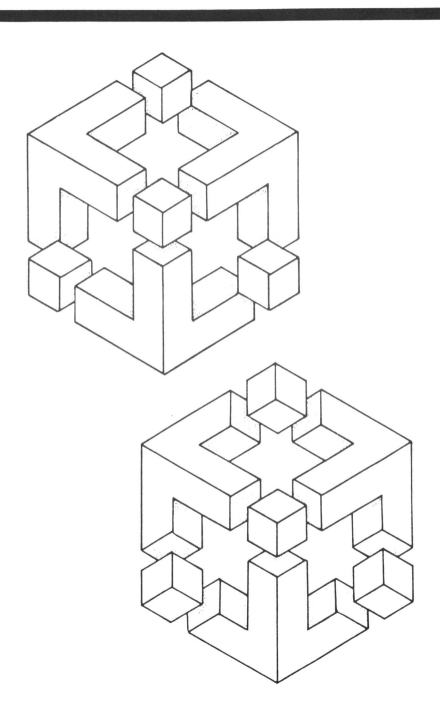

Impossible Windows

For these drawings I started with an ordinary window frame and then experimented with different kinds of impossible connections.

The figure on this page shows what happens when you try to combine a view through a window with an impossible figure. For me, the tension between the two aspects is very strong and I can scarecly see the frame at all. The rural scene seems to take all of my attention and it is difficult to notice the impossibility of its surroundings. Do try experimenting with different window frames and different photographs.

'Ascending and Descending' by Escher(1960)

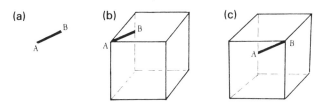

(a)   (b)   (c)

When we look at a drawing of a line segment entirely on its own, we cannot know what it represents. In (a) the line segment AB looks straight and it might be a line. However, it could even be a circle seen sideways in the plane of the observer. We cannot tell. Even if we know that it is a straight line, we still cannot say what its orientation in space is. If the context is as in (b), then A is higher and nearer than B. In (c), A is further away and lower than B. Yet in all three cases the actual marks AB on the paper are identical in size and direction.

The addition of an extra line segment to AB does give more information, especially if it is repeated several times. However, more of the context is necessary before we can be sure what is meant.

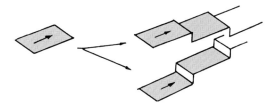

There is no doubt in these sketches that one set of stairs leads upwards and the other leads downwards. The repeated and joined line segments are supported with other visual information to make a convincing impression.

'Ascending and Descending'

That both kinds of staircase could be combined to make a new impossible figure was first put forward by L.S. & R. Penrose in 1958. In the article which also introduced the impossible tri-bar, they explained how a staircase could rise or fall endlessly and yet return to the same level. Escher borrowed the idea and produced the splendid lithograph'ASCENDING AND DESCENDING'(1960) which is shown opposite. The hooded figures toil endlessly upwards and downwards, clockwise and anticlockwise, lost in thought about the impossibility of their situation.

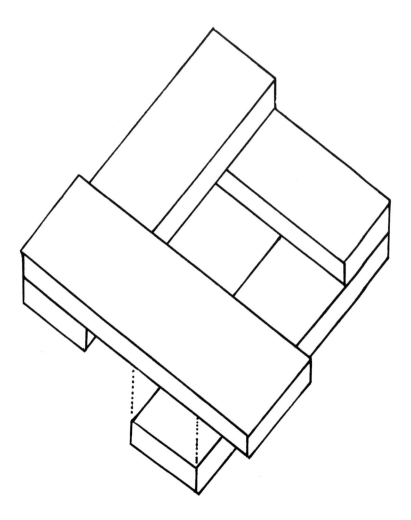

Since a drawing of the tread of a staircase has no sense of direction, we must introduce other visual signposts to indicate whether the stairway leads upwards or downwards. This drawing shows a stairway which descends in a clockwise direction using only four steps. As a result there is a gap of two stair heights when the circuit is completed. All the visual indicators are consistent and there is no impossibility.

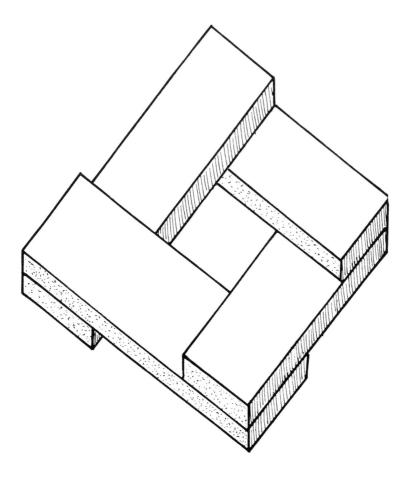

The drawing opposite has now been modified to introduce false indicators and as a result we have created an impossible staircase with only four treads. Descend in a clockwise direction. Ascend in an anticlockwise direction. Follow the mysterious stairway which leads to nowhere at all!

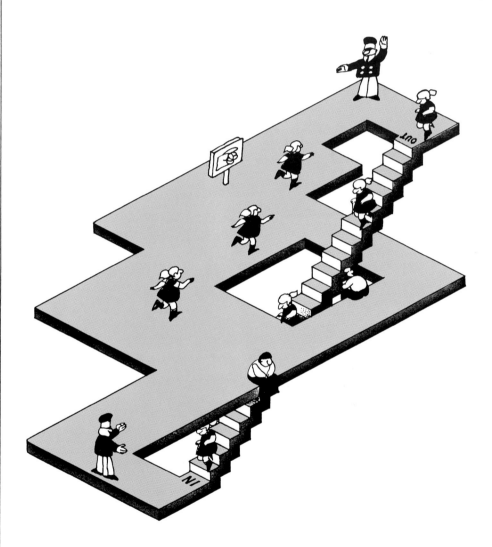

This is an adaptation of one of Oscar Reutersvärd's many drawings of impossible staircases. The top stairs of a long staircase is reconnected to the bottom stair by a flat plane. I have added figures and signs to accentuate the contradiction of 'up' and 'down', 'in' and 'out'. The behaviour of the figures draws attention to the fact that there is no possible escape, although some appear not to have realised it yet. The men gave up a long time ago!

The Greeks were renowned for their power of abstract thought. But is the problem posed by this drawing too much even for them ? Would it give a Caryatid a headache ?

Level and yet Rising

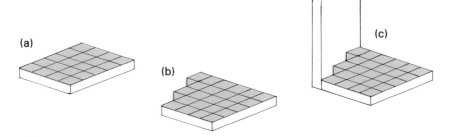

These three drawings show just how influenced we are by the clues and visual signposts which tell us of position in space. In (a) we have no difficulty in interpreting it as a flat plane divided into square tiles.In (b) the far edge could be jagged, although the eye is rather tempted to perceive them as steps. In (c) we have added further indications of a vertical wall and the eye jumps to the conclusion that there is indeed a rising staircase. Of course that then raises the problem of explaining how it is that the right hand edge is still flat!

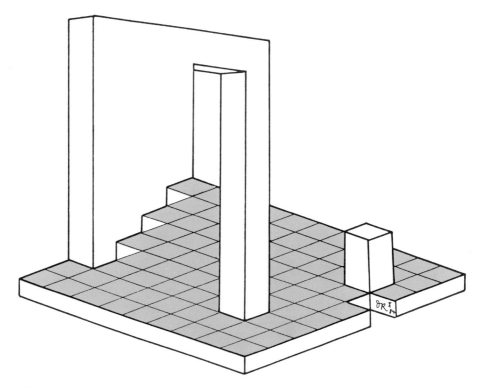

Add a few more details and we have a delightfully impossible figure.

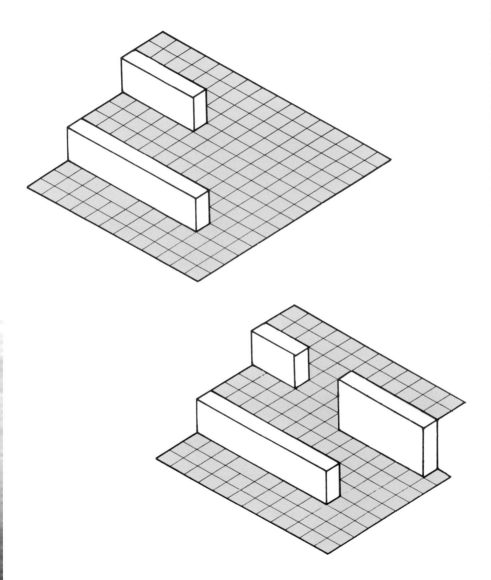

Here are further experiments with tiled floors which have produced two more impossible figures.

Let us now look back at Escher's 'WATERFALL' on page 17. Notice how he has indicated which way the water must flow by making the sides of the channel step downwards as an impossible stairway.

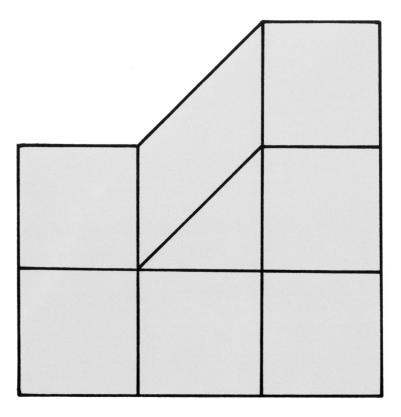

The success with square tiles in the previous section suggested that it would be interesting to experiment with a chess-board and see if any new intriguing figures could be devised. This proved to be the case and it was not difficult to make some convincing impossible figures, this time in photographic form. The effect seems to demand remarkably few squares and only two squares have had to be modified. I hope that you agree that the effect is quite strong.

Opposite is a real photograph of a perfectly flat board. The queen is both higher than her subjects and on exactly the same level!

The queen stands on the same level as the rook and higher than the pawn. But the rook and the pawn stand at the same level.

Photographing the chess-board and its reflection in a mirror does not destroy the illusion at all.

7. Planes, Far and Near at the Same Time

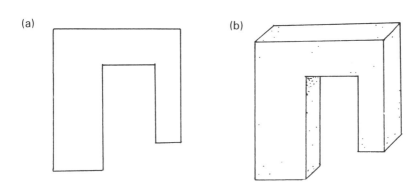

(a)

(b)

The inverted U shape in (a) is undoubtedly flat. In (b) it has a thickness, but it is clear than the front plane is still near to us and is still flat. We can also easily believe that the far side of this solid shape is also flat, although we have no evidence for this beyond the horizontal and vertical edges which are visible.

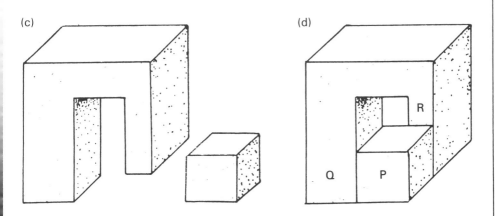

(c)

(d)

In (c) the shape has become thicker and a small cube has appeared on the scene. Still no problem. In (d) the cube has moved and immediately there is a conflict. P and Q are the same distance from us and so are Q and R. But P is definitely nearer than R. We have a figure where a plane appears to be at two different distances from the viewpoint, both at the same time. The result is impossibility.

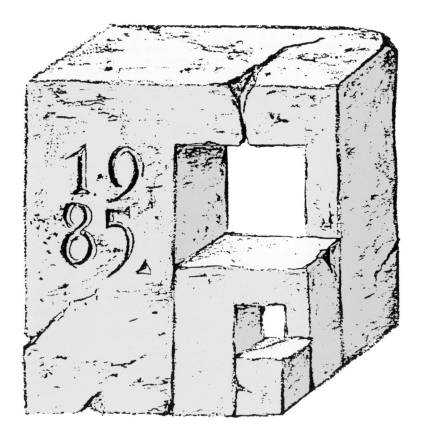

We can make a further impossible figure out of the small cube by using a still smaller cube. So the process could continue step by step for ever.... But perhaps three steps are enough for the moment!

We can pursue the same kind of game with three or more pillars which have a beam resting on them. Notice how the massive beam and the massive base establish a very strong sense of reality, which is then disturbed by the position of the feet of the pillars. Compare this figure with the one on page 66. The Belgian artist Jos de Mey has painted a great number of extraordinarily realistic paintings on this theme, inspired by the paintings of Magritte.

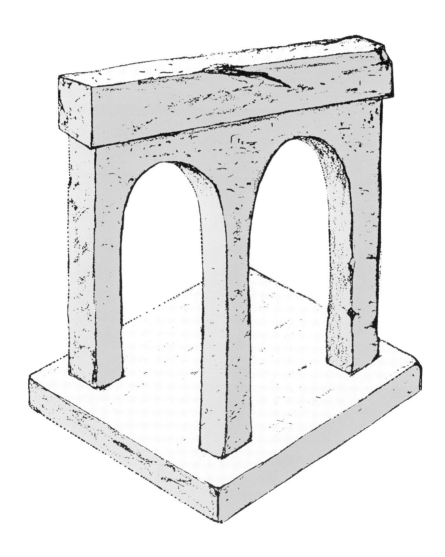

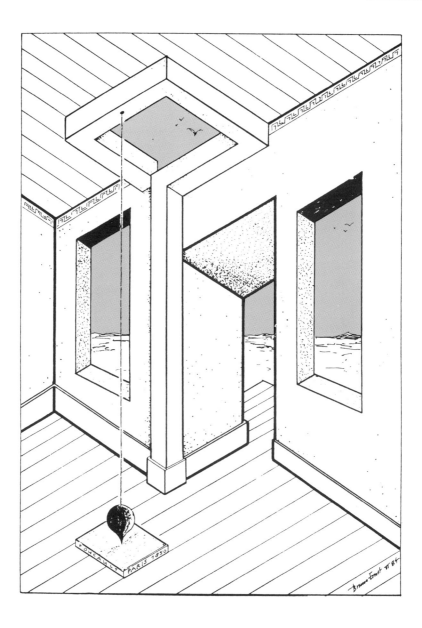

The thick wall with the doorway in it lies at two different distances from us. Drawings of this kind are made more interesting by introducing special details. Here a Foucault pendulum gives a very strong sense of the vertical direction.

"All right! All right! I know you built this from the first draft of the plans for the Parthenon. I'm only saying that there must be some reason why the Ancient Greeks threw them away!"

An Example from the Fifteenth Century

In 1902, during the restoration of the Grote Kerk in Breda in Holland, a fifteenth century impossible figure was discovered. It is the earliest one so far known and it shows the Archangel Gabriel telling Mary of her future Son. The scene is framed by the two arches, supported by three pillars. The two outside pillars are in the foreground whereas the middle pillar disappears behind a table. There is an obvious practical need to use an impossible figure like this because the painter did not want the scene to be divided into two separate halves.

The art historian J. Kalf described this picture in his book 'De monumenten de voormalige Baronie van Breda', published in Utrecht in 1912. He wrote:- ''The picture shows a room divided into two halves by a (perspectively misplaced) red pillar with a grey capital....''

He described the impossibility as 'misplaced perspective'. How else could he have described it at a time years before impossible figures became accepted as having a reality of their own? We shall never know if the artist was having trouble in dealing with the laws of perspective or if he did consciously decide to draw an impossible figure. It would be nice to think he did!

This drawing was inspired by the mural opposite and the idea of the impossible arch has been used more than once.

The Carceri by Piranesi

In 1760 a collection of lithographs by Giovanni Battista Piranesi was published which was called 'Carceri d'invenzione' or 'imaginary dungeons'. This was an adaption of an earlier series of lithographs made in 1745.

Many writers have puzzled over these strange scenes and spatially mysterious images. Piranesi has not left us any clues to help understand them, but it does appear that he used impossible figures, either consciously or unconsciously.

This illustration is the left side of print XIV.

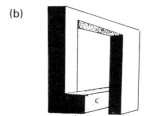

Figure (a) shows a very simplified diagram of the print. The impossibility occurs between A and B where the bridge marked C disappears behind the second pillar. Figure (b) shows the essence of the impossibility where the A,B,C correspond with the letters in (a).

Rudy Kousboek brought this print to my attention and described this detail as an impossible four-bar. In my opinion this is not exactly the case, but they are strongly connected.

8. Both Horizontal and Vertical

In the real world a flat surface cannot be both horizontal and vertical at the same time. Everyone knows that and so perhaps this would be a good new area to explore in our search for new impossible figures.

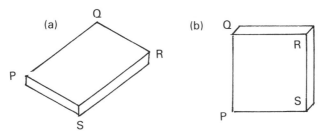

We have no problem in seeing drawing (a) as a sketch of a horizontal surface. In (b) the surface PQRS seems to be vertical. Can we combine the two?

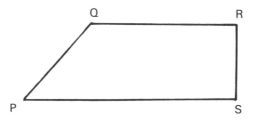

Let us now look carefully at the trapezium PQRS. Notice how we have taken the direction of PQ from (a) and the direction of RS from (b). If we concentrate on the left hand edge of the drawing it is possible to interpret it as a horizontal plane. The right hand edge could be a vertical plane. Can we force both interpretations at the same time by adding more and contradictory visual signposts?

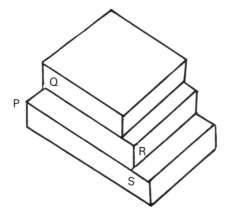

The solidity of the blocks forces us to see PQ as horizontal and RS as vertical in spite of the fact that PQRS is a trapezium. The same plane is both horizontal and vertical at the same time and we can add another new impossible figure to our collection!

A Temple to Impossibility?

Many people have devised impossible drawings where a plane or planes can be seen as horizontal and vertical at the same time. I discovered this interesting variation only recently. It is an impossible step-pyramid where the number of steps seems to grow in an almost miraculous way. On the left side there are three steps, in the centre five and on the right there are nine. Yet each interpretation seems totally convincing within its own region of the figure. All steps lead upwards to the temple on top. Is this not the perfect design for a temple to impossibility?

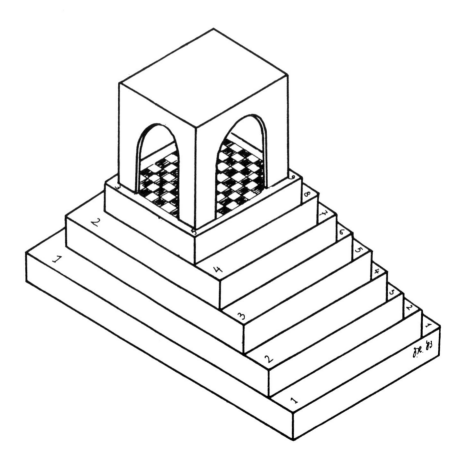

All steps are equal, but some are more equal than others!

The three sketches on this page show the three elements from which the figure opposite was built. None is impossible and you can climb up to each real temple by using three, five or nine real stairs.

This figure shows an impossible temple drawn with perspective. Most of the illustrations in this book have been drawn using an isometric projection and true perspective has largely been ignored. This has meant that parallel lines have been drawn parallel and not converging to a vanishing point. We have also ignored the fact that in a perspective drawing objects which are further away must be drawn smaller. Curiously, the eye does not seem very sensitive to these indicators of position in space, at least for the kind of figures we have met in this book.

It is worth looking back at pages 20 and 74 to see figures in which different kinds of isometric projection have been used for the walls and for the ceilings. In both drawings it was important to include both the ceiling and the floor in order to strengthen the feeling of false perspective which so adds to the strangeness of the rooms.

9. Disappearing Spaces

In this chapter we deal with a new class of impossible figures, where the principle is rather different from anything which has gone before.

Is the candlestick drawn below a sketch of a candlestick which could really exist?

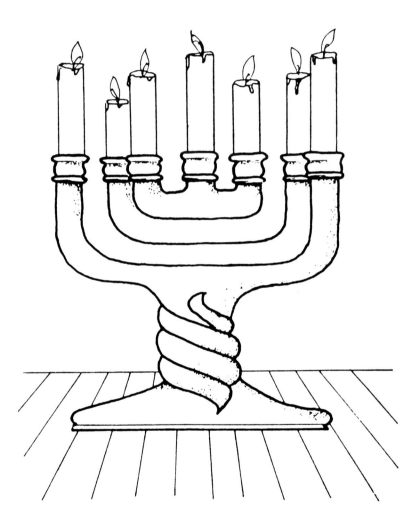

When you look carefully at this candlestick, I am sure that you will agree that in certain places it seems to dissolve away to nothing. Where did the holder of the second candle from the right go to? And the second from the left?
Let us now see what we can find which behaves in a similar and impossible way.

Disappearing Blocks

This figure has a strong sense of solidity about it. Both at the bottom and at the top there appear to be three solid blocks. Yet there are problems. block B undoubtedly exists at the bottom, but as we raise our eyes it just vanishes into nothingness. Block C exists at the top, but it vanishes lower down.

Block A appears to be normal and block D is a variation on the ideas of chapter 8. It is on B and C that we must concentrate.

What then is the trick of the vanishing blocks based on? Let us look at the line PQ. It serves a double function. It is the edge of both block A and of block B. Real objects have real boundaries and that is what we expect to see. Our eye does not have to see a complete outline before starting to interpret it as a solid object. Near to the letter Q the outline of B suggests a solid block. By the time we reach P it has disappeared and that is what causes the shock.

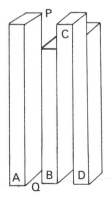

This modified sketch completes the outlines of block B and so the sense of vanishing into thin air has also disappeared. However, other kinds of impossibility still remain to tease the imagination!

Dual-purpose Outlines

The eye automatically uses the outlines of figures to acquire information about planes and their orientation in space. Where the same outline apparently belongs to two different objects, then there can be deliberate confusion. However, the strong sense of confusion that a dual-purpose outline can create is not confined to three-dimensional impossible figures.

This well-known two-dimensional figure allows two quite different interpretations. Is it a vase, or is it two faces facing each other? It is not an impossible figure, but is closer to the phenomenon of perceptual inversion of chapter 4. It is either a vase or it is a pair of faces. Not both.

Things are not Always What They Seem.

The technique of the disappearing outline is one which can produce a whole range of interesting impossible drawings. On the pages which follow we show just a few ideas.

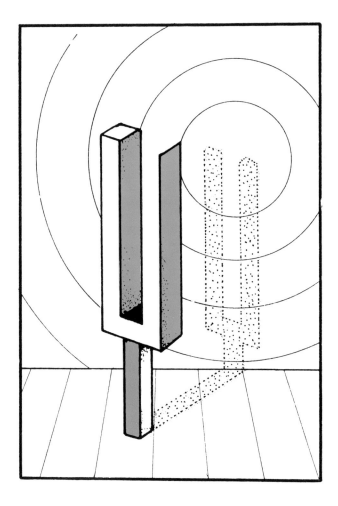

This impossible tuning fork seems to cast a real shadow on the back wall. And of course it is the shadow, not the fork, which emits the soundless sound waves!

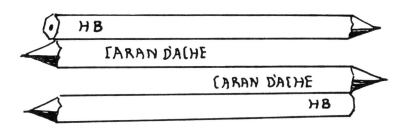

Disappearing ink is supposedly much beloved by spies and crooked business men. Are these the first disappearing pencils for artists to use to create invisible masterpieces? Were they used to draw the three pictures on the walls of the art gallery on page 22?

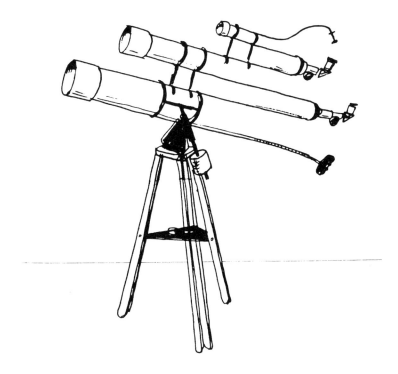

Astronomers often use a small 'finder' scope to point a powerful telescope at a faint object in the night sky. Could the telescope drawn here by Govert Schilling be used to give a clear view of something totally invisible?

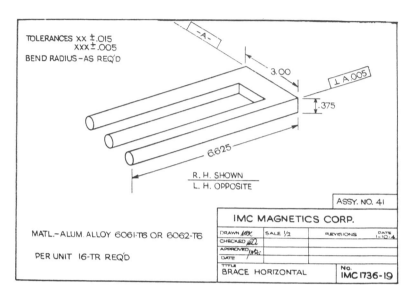

TOLERANCES XX ±.015
          XXX±.005
BEND RADIUS –AS REQ'D

-A-

3.00

⊥ A .005

.375

6.625

R. H. SHOWN
L. H. OPPOSITE

ASSY. NO. 41

IMC MAGNETICS CORP.			
DRAWN *IRK*	SALE ½	REVISIONS	DATE 1-10-4
CHECKED			
APPROVED			
DATE			
TITLE BRACE HORIZONTAL		No. IMC 1736-19	

MATL.– ALUM. ALLOY 6061-T6 OR 6062-T6

PER UNIT 16-TR REQ'D

"The difficult we do immediately. The impossible takes a little longer".
However, the provision of accurate blue-prints does speed up the process!

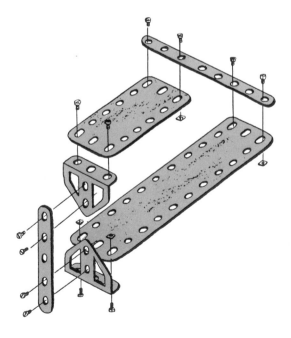

Is it possible that this Meccano enthusiast has a screw loose?

Things are indeed not always what they seem!

10. A Test for Impossibility?

If we draw a figure which cannot actually exist in space, is it always obvious that we have done so? Is there a simple test which we could apply which would tell us with certainty whether or not a particular figure is impossible?

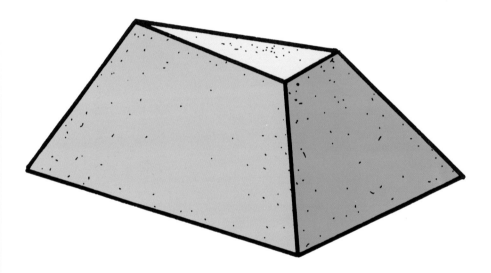

Most people would be able to accept this as a sketch of a real truncated pyramid. Yet I can tell you that it is really an impossible figure and prove it to your satisfaction. Can you see how? The solution is given on page 94, but do try to find it yourself first.

In order to decide about certain figures it seems that we cannot rely on the automatic response of the eye. We need to think, to reason and to try to find a method or test which would help us to make the correct decision.

The drawing above is not an impossible figure, but it does demonstrate how the automatic response of the eye is dulled once the drawing becomes too complicated. The figure consists of a single long and narrow loop which has been folded up in a manner reminiscent of the intestines. The problem is to decide whether A is inside or outside the loop.

To solve it we have to do more than just look. We have to reason. One way to decide would be to treat it like a maze problem and to try to find a route to the outside. If we can find no route to the outside, then we could say that A must be inside. However, most of us have had difficulty with maze problems in the past and the doubt would always remain that there might be a yet undiscovered route which would work.

For this problem there is a better solution. Let us draw any line, straight or curved, from A to the outside. For example, see AB above. Now let us count the number of lines we cross. Every time we cross a line, we are either crossing from the inside to the outside or from the outside to the inside. An even number of crossings on the route to the outside must mean that A is outside the loop. An odd number means that A is inside. Using this simple test, it is very easy to make the correct decision.

This problem was chosen as an example because it does have solutions on different levels and with different degrees of certainty. Perhaps we could use the insights so gained to devise a test which we could apply to impossible figures?

Many people have tried to devise a simple test like the one on the previous page, but so far without total success. Some tests appear to apply only to specific figures like the tri-bar, four-bar or multi-bar.

Perhaps you might like to experiment with the following test.

Draw or imagine a plane cutting through the figure. The line on each drawing represents the plane, although the plane does not necessarily have to be at right-angles to the paper. Cover the part of the figure to one side of the line with a piece of paper. Then sketch the cross-section which the plane makes with that part of the figure which remains. Then cover the other half and sketch that cross-section.

If both sketches are identical, then the figure is possible. If they are different in any respect, then it is impossible.

To illustrate how it works, here are five examples. Four of them are impossible and one is possible.

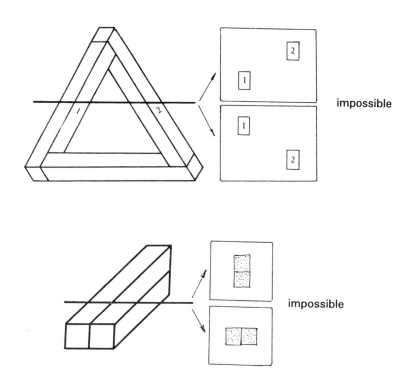

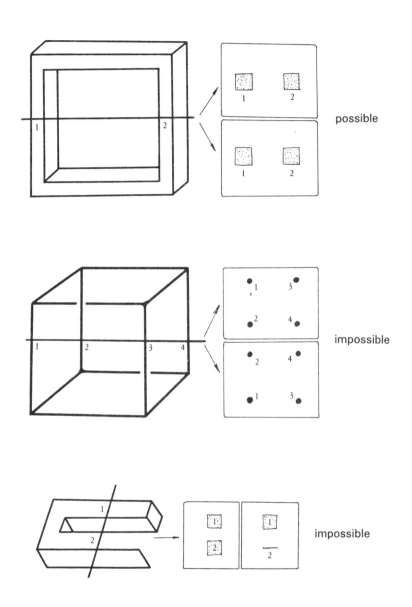

This method still demands a good understanding of each figure which is being tested and does require an element of subjective judgement. It does not work very well on figures like the one on page 90 where the impossibility is not very great. However, I hope that it will point the way one day towards a really satisfactory solution to this tricky problem.

Something Unique

The study of impossible figures has added something new and unique to the visual world of man. It offers an enrichment of the human spirit and a valuable field for the human imagination to explore. It is certainly not a branch of mathematics, although mathematical methods can be used to describe and analyse the figures. Nor is it necessarily art. Impossible figures can be drawn in a harmonious and expressive way, but they can just as well be rather ugly. They do awaken a response in most people, a certain sense of wonder — and they certainly help us in our attempt to understand how the eye-brain combination processes visual information. In so doing it may well help with the development of programs which would enable computer controlled robots to 'see'. Perhaps it is not surprising that of more than one hundred articles written about impossible figures since 1970, most of them have been published in computer magazines.

Solution to the problem on page 91

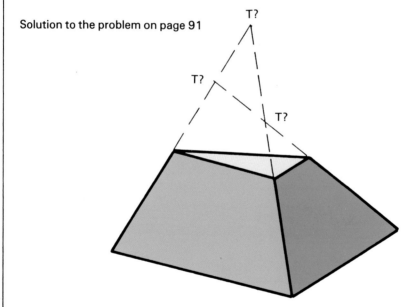

Continuing the three lines of the sides of the pyramid leads to three different places, each of which must be the vertex. Hence it must be an impossible figure.

Bibliography

It is outside the scope of this book to give a complete list of the books and articles which have been written about impossible figures.

We name in particular one remarkable and readable article, which has an extensive bibliography.

Z.Kulpa: Are impossible figures possible?: Signal Processing, vol. 5, no.3,(1983), 201-220.

The six books listed below contain a great number of works of art based on impossible figures.

Sandro del Prete : Illusorismen : Bentelli Verlag, Bern (3rd impression) 1984

Franco Grignani : A methodology of vision : Milan 1975.

Mitsumasa Anno : Jeux de construction : L'Ecole, Paris 1970

Toshihiro Katayama : Visual construction, square movement, topology, hommage to the cube : Tokyo 1981.

Oscar Reutersvärd : Onmogelijke figuren : Meulenhoff/Landshoff, Amsterdam 1983

Oscar Reutersvärd : Onmöjliga figurer i färg : Doxa, Lund 1985.
(This book is a different collection from the previous book).

Other Books by Bruno Ernst

The Magic Mirror of M.C.Escher : Tarquin 1986 (reprint of Ballantine 1976)
M.C.Escher, his life and complete graphic work : Abrams, New York.(co-author)

An up to date catalogue of books published by Tarquin may be obtained from Tarquin Publications, Stradbroke, Diss, Norfolk IP21 5JP. Tel.037 984 218.